AF382270

THE CONSTRUCTION OF THE EUROPEAN UNION

Working for Peace and Prosperity in Europe

Written by Pierre Mettra
In collaboration with Romain Prévalet
Translated by Rebecca Neal

History 50MINUTES.com

THE CONSTRUCTION OF THE EUROPEAN UNION

KEY INFORMATION

- **When:** 1945-present.
- **Context:** in the aftermath of the Second World War, there was a strong desire to restore peace in Europe and to foster strong continent-wide economic, political and diplomatic cooperation.
- **Key protagonists:**
  - Konrad Adenauer (Chancellor of the Federal Republic of Germany, 1876-1967).
  - Robert Schuman (French politician, 1886-1963).
  - Jean Monnet (French administrator and President of the High Authority of the European Coal and Steel Community, 1888-1979).
  - Charles de Gaulle (President of France, 1890-1970).
  - Paul-Henri Spaak (Prime Minister of Belgium, 1899-1972).

- ○ François Mitterrand (President of France, 1916-1996).
  - ○ Valéry Giscard d'Estaing (President of France, born in 1926).
  - ○ Helmut Kohl (Chancellor of Germany, 1930-2017).
- **Impact:** the creation of a European institution to facilitate cooperation across a range of economic, political and social sectors.

INTRODUCTION

Every five years, elections are held for the citizens of Europe to choose their representatives in the European Parliament. The last elections, which took place in May 2014, saw an average abstention rate of 59%. One possible reason for this low turnout is a lack of clarity about how the EU actually works: the organisation has existed for decades and undergone a number of shifts during that time, leaving many people with questions and doubts about how it functions.

Nonetheless, the idea behind the EU could not be simpler. In the aftermath of the Second World War (1939-1945), key European leaders wanted to set the continent on the path to recovery and prevent the outbreak of any further conflicts. In their opinion, the way forward was to bring the countries of Europe together within an organisation based on cooperation. Europe's political and intellectual elites approved of the project and developed an ideological definition of Europe, which they viewed as an essentially Catholic civilisation.

In the early 1950s, in a world divided by the first major tensions of the Cold War (1945-1990), European integration was viewed as a way for the continent to find its place in the new world order, where empires were crumbling and power was split between the American-dominated West and the Soviet-led East. The fall of the Berlin Wall in 1989 marked a major shift and paved the way for countries from the former Eastern bloc to enter the European collective. Now, the organisation was not just about strength in numbers, but also about sustainable international cooperation across a range of sectors. On the basis of past experience, there was a move towards greater federalism, which had previously been roundly rejected. A telling illustration of this new, broader outlook is the shift from the European Economic Community to the European Union.

After a period of stability, recent events, namely the popular referendum in June 2016 in which UK citizens voted to leave the EU and the rise of far-right and Eurosceptic parties across Europe, have inaugurated a time of far greater uncertainty. Indeed, since its inception, the EU has met with sometimes virulent criticism, inspired in large part by the fear that cooperation between the nations of Europe poses a threat to each country's national sovereignty. In this guide, we will examine how the European Union came to assume its current form, how it functions and what the future may hold.

POLITICAL, SOCIAL AND ECONOMIC CONTEXT

EARLY EXPERIMENTS IN COOPERATION (1945-1957)

The first steps towards closer collaboration between Europe's politicians took place immediately after the end of the Second World War. Indeed, if they wanted to recover from the extensive destruction and profound trauma engendered by the conflict, they had no choice but to work together, and were encouraged to do so by the USA. This was a vital step, because stronger economies and social bonds were a prerequisite for the construction of a united Europe.

Rebuilding a war-torn continent

In the years immediately after the war, Europe was at its lowest ebb: the material damage sustained by most of the countries that had fought in the war led to a drop in production, which in turn meant that many products were next to impossible to get hold of, giving rise to a substantial black market. This was accompanied by high rates of inflation, which served to compound the continent's economic problems. In short, Europe needed to be completely rebuilt, but its countries lacked the resources to do so.

The USA was eager to assist Europe in its reconstruction, motivated not only by a desire to ensure sustainable peace between the former warring countries, but also by its own political interests. The US government was worried by the advance of Soviet forces in Eastern Europe, and President Harry S. Truman (1884-1972), whose policy of containment sought to halt the spread of Communism, wanted to create a strong democratic bloc in Europe to counter the USSR's expansion. Furthermore, the continent's economic recovery would provide the USA with trading partners and kick-start the global economy. Consequently, Truman rejected a plan to force the defeated Germany to pay for the damage inflicted in the course of the war and opted instead for the Marshall Plan in 1947, which had been devised by the Secretary of State George Marshall (1880-1959) and involved providing aid to the European countries for free.

The Organisation for European Economic Cooperation and the Western European Union

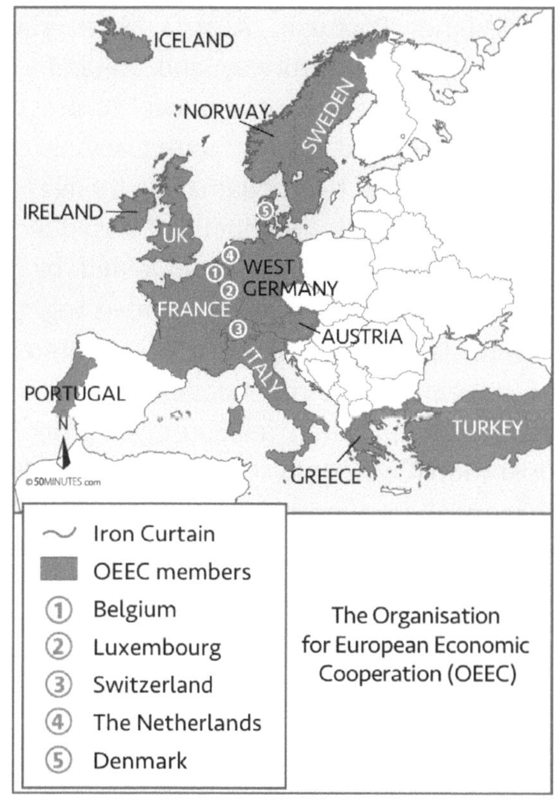

The Organisation for European Economic Cooperation (OEEC)

The first step was to find out which countries wanted to receive American aid and set up a transnational organisation to distribute it. France and the UK were immediately eager to participate, and they were joined by Belgium, Luxembourg, the Netherlands, Greece, Turkey, Italy, Ireland, Portugal, Austria, Switzerland, Denmark, Sweden, Norway and Iceland. The countries of Eastern Europe bowed to pressure from the USSR and did not accept any aid, nor did Finland, out of fear of damaging its relations with its powerful neighbour. Consequently, 16 countries, which were later joined by the Federal Republic of Germany, banded together to receive US funds. Following the Conference on European Economic Cooperation held in Paris, the Organisation for European Economic Cooperation (OEEC) was created on 16 April 1948 to manage these funds. This was the first formal attempt at cooperation in Europe, and aimed to help its members integrate into a liberal economy, funded by the American Marshall Plan.

The OEEC's Secretariat was based at the Château de Muette in Paris. The organisation comprised a Council with representatives from each member state and an Executive Committee whose members were selected by the Council. From its inception in 1948 until 1960, when it was superseded by the Organisation for Economic Cooperation and Development (OECD), the OEEC fostered trade between the European nations.

At the same time, the countries of Europe were worried by the mounting tensions between the Western and Eastern blocs. The UK and France, with the backing of the USA, began to consider a pact to create a European military alliance, which would be useful if war broke out in the East. They were soon joined by Belgium, Luxembourg and the Netherlands, and on 17 March 1948, these five countries signed the Treaty of Brussels, which created the Western European Union (WEU). The treaty made provisions for collaboration across a range of sectors, but was primarily focused on collective defence. Specifically, it stipulated the creation of a Consultative Council headquartered in London which would bring together the foreign ministers of the member states and a joint general staff.

However, the OEEC and WEU did not bring

about true political unity between the countries of Europe. The fact that the treaty portrayed Germany as a potential aggressor is a clear sign of the work that still needed to be done to foster mutual trust and ensure sustainable peace in a united Europe.

The Congress of Europe

The aftermath of the Second World War saw the emergence of numerous international associations whose aim was to build a federated Europe, the most prominent of which included the Union of European Federalists and the United Europe Movement. These groups counted among their members influential figures such as the Belgian prime minister Paul-Henri Spaak and the Italian thinker Altiero Spinelli (1907-1986), one of the coauthors of the *Ventotene Manifesto* (1941), which challenged the concept of a national state and advocated the construction of a European federation.

These various associations were fertile ground for new ideas about the future of Europe, and sought to form a structured collective. The first step towards doing so was to develop a liaison body and organise a meeting bringing together the most important figures involved in the nascent European project. To this end, the Congress of Europe was held in The Hague from 7 to 10 May 1948, presided over by the former British prime minister Winston Churchill (1874-1965). Many European countries attended, as did Canada and the USA in an observatory capacity. A number of ambitious projects were conceived during the conference, and working groups were set up to develop concrete plans and draw up a proposal to present to the member countries of the OEEC. In addition, the Congress of Europe formally brought together the continent's various pro-Europe associations as part of a broader structure that made coordination easier, the European Movement.

The report presented to the OEEC on 18 August 1948 represented the first project for European cooperation with federalist leanings. Specifically, this text advocated the creation of a Europe-wide consultative assembly tasked with fostering economic and legal integration across the continent. France was the first country to respond to this proposal: at a meeting of the five signatories of the Treaty of Brussels, the country's foreign minister, Georges Bidault (1899-1983), suggested creating this assembly and establishing an economic and customs union. When Bidault left his post shortly afterwards, it was left to his successor Robert Schuman to bring the project to fruition.

KEY PROTAGONISTS

KONRAD ADENAUER

Konrad Adenauer was born in Cologne in 1976, and went on to become the first Chancellor of the Federal Republic of Germany after the war. He faced a number of major challenges in this role, namely winning the trust of Germany's neighbours, forging closer bonds between his country and the West, and dealing with the division of Germany into two states aligned with opposing blocs. He was a firm believer in the European project, which he saw as a way to both achieve his personal objectives and guarantee lasting peace on the continent. Modern-day Germany owes a great deal to his skilful leadership between 1949 and 1963.

ROBERT SCHUMAN

Robert Schuman was born in Luxembourg in 1886 and spent part of his childhood in Lorraine, which at that time belonged to Germany. When Lorraine was restored to France in 1918, Schuman embarked on a political career and occupied a series of increasingly important posts. He joined the French government in 1940 and remained in his position throughout the Second World War. In 1947, he was appointed prime minister, then foreign minister. Having grown up in a border region and been both a German and a French citizen, Schuman was convinced of the need for a sustainable union in Europe. He was president of the European Movement from 1955 to 1961 and served a two-year term as the first President of the European Parliament, beginning in 1958. His initiatives led to the creation of the European Coal and Steel Community (ECSC), which paved the way for the construction of the European Union.

JEAN MONNET

Jean Monnet was born in Cognac, southwestern France, in 1888, and by the time projects to build a united Europe were getting underway he had already amassed a great deal of political experience, particularly in the field of international cooperation. In 1916, when he occupied a high-ranking position at the Ministry of Commerce, he set up a committee to coordinate resources between the Allied powers. In 1940, while he was in exile in London, he drew up a plan for France and Britain to pool their resources. He was firmly committed to the European project, and his actions strengthened economic cooperation between the continent's various countries.

CHARLES DE GAULLE

General de Gaulle, who was born in Lille in 1890, served as the leader of Free France, and in this capacity played a vital role in organising the Resistance to the German occupation of France. After the Liberation, he became the head of the Provisional Government of the French Republic until 1946. He then took some time away from politics, before being elected President of France on 21 December 1958.

De Gaulle and Adenauer worked together towards a rapprochement between France and Germany, with the aim of improving international relations across Europe. However, he was opposed to the idea of a supranational Europe and exercised his right to veto on a number of occasions, meaning that there was little progress in terms of European cooperation during his presidency.

PAUL-HENRI SPAAK

Paul-Henri Spaak was born in 1899 in Schaerbeek (Brussels region), and went on to play an important role in the Belgian government in exile during the Second World War. In 1946 he became President of the United Nations General Assembly, while also holding ministerial positions in the Belgian government. He was a passionate believer in the construction of a united Europe, and as the Belgian foreign minister, he made a major contribution to this project. He led the European Movement between 1950 and 1955 and represented Belgium at the signing of the Treaty of Rome on 25 March 1957, which brought the European Economic Community (EEC) into existence.

FRANÇOIS MITTERRAND

The French socialist politician François Mitterrand was born in Jarnac, southwestern France, in 1916 and was elected president in 1981. He worked in partnership with Helmut Kohl's

government to strengthen European cooperation, and was the first French leader to accept
the European Parliament's proposal to make
greater use of majority decisions in the European
institutions.

VALÉRY GISCARD D'ESTAING

Valéry Giscard d'Estaing was born in 1926 in
Koblenz, a German city that was at that time
under French control. He supported closer
European integration in the belief that this was
the key to effective political management. For
this reason, he was the driving force behind
the first meeting of the five most industrialised
countries in 1975, which could be compared to a
sort of early G5.

From 1989 to 1997, he served as president of the
European Movement International, and from
2001 to 2004 he presided over the Convention on
the Future of Europe, which drafted the Treaty
establishing a Constitution for Europe. Although
the treaty was passed by the European Council, it
never entered into force as it was not ratified by
all member states.

HELMUT KOHL

Helmut Kohl was born in Ludwigshafen in 1930 and became Chancellor of Germany in 1982. He embraced the idea of European integration and, thanks to his partnership with François Mitterrand, was a major driving force behind greater cooperation across the continent. He also played a role in German reunification in 1990 with the support of the European Community, in particular in exchange for membership of the Economic and Monetary Union (EMU).

THE CONSTRUCTION OF THE EU

THE CREATION OF THE COUNCIL OF EUROPE

When he became the French foreign minister, Robert Schuman embraced the European Movement's suggestion of establishing a consultative European assembly, and on 18 August 1947 the French government gave the project its approval. France's political class viewed Germany's integration with the rest of Europe as the best way to avert the rise of nationalism in the country and embed its economy within Western Europe. Once the French government had passed this proposal, Schuman informed his European counterparts of the decision with a view to opening discussions. The first of these took place between the five signatories of the Treaty of Brussels, namely France, the UK, Belgium, the Netherlands and Luxembourg.

For its part, Germany welcomed these suggestions, and the country's Chancellor Konrad Adenauer, a member of the liberal-conservative Christian Democratic Union of Germany, encouraged the new project. He believed that his country's recovery depended on close collaboration with the other European countries, particularly France. Germany was still in turmoil following the Second World War, which meant that it could not join the association at this time, although its future membership was already on the table.

This enthusiasm for the European project was shared by the government of Paul-Henri Spaak, a member of the European Movement, in Belgium. However, the UK government was much more reticent, as it opposed the creation of specific institutions for European cooperation and refused to countenance any steps that could lead to supranationalism.

WHAT IS SUPRANATIONALISM?

Supranationalism means that an international organisation has more power than its member countries. In this situation, the nations do not retain all their sovereign rights, because some of these are held by the supranational organisation. This means that if an EU member state passes new national laws, it must respect EU directives, even if this means modifying its own legislative texts. For example, an EU country could not reintroduce the death penalty. The concept of supranationalism therefore stands in opposition to nationalism, which promotes total national sovereignty.

Subsequent discussions, which also included Ireland, Italy, Norway, Sweden and Denmark, led to a compromise. The Treaty of London was signed by ten nations on 5 May 1949 and created the Council of Europe, comprising two institutions based in Strasbourg: a consultative assembly made up of delegates selected by the member countries, and a committee of the foreign ministers of each country, whose role is to draw up recommendations for the member states based on suggestions made by the assembly. The Council's aim is to encourage European cooperation across more sectors and to ensure that human rights and the rule of law are respected across the continent. The new body complied with the UK's demands, but was not completely in line with Schuman's ideas. Along with Jean Monnet, who was at that time the head of France's Plan Commission (the organisation in charge of the country's economic planning), he embarked on a more ambitious project.

THE EUROPEAN COAL AND STEEL COMMUNITY: TOWARDS ECONOMIC INTEGRATION

Jean Monnet was a liberal politician, and harboured dreams of a strong federal Europe. However, this could only be achieved through a commercial union of the countries of Europe. Monnet believed that steel, a key economic sector, would be a good starting point, and in April 1950 he developed a project proposing a European economic association focusing on cooperation in steel production. When Monnet contacted Schuman, he was immediately won over by the idea. As France's foreign minister, he threw his support behind the project in the Council of Ministers and managed to persuade the French government to accept it.

Negotiations immediately began between the countries interested in the proposal, which quickly became known as the Schuman Plan. It was received enthusiastically by Luxembourg and Italy, and by the German Chancellor Konrad Adenauer, while Belgium and the Netherland were more reluctant as they feared that they would struggle to weather competition in the steel and coal sectors. However, the UK government rejected the plan outright because it involved the creation of a High Authority, a supranational institution which would have decision-making powers and whose members would work exclusively towards its own interests.

Consequently, on 18 April 1951 six countries signed the Treaty of Paris, which created the European Coal and Steel Community (ECSC) for a 50-year period. This organisation aimed to guarantee peace between the countries of Europe and to implement joint economic management which would both stimulate the continent's economic recovery and ensure decent working conditions for employees. It also created the first European supranational institution, the High Authority which had inspired such staunch opposition from the UK government. It initially comprised nine members from the six signatories of the treaty, who were tasked with providing opinions and making enforceable decisions. A Common Assembly, comprising 78 members, met once per year to examine the report produced by the High Authority and, if necessary, to oppose its decisions. Furthermore, the High Authority needed the approval of a Special Commission of Ministers if it wished to make a decision that was not connected to the coal and steel sectors. Finally, if a member state disagreed with the decisions of the High Authority, it could appeal to a Court of Justice comprised of seven judges.

Monnet and Schuman's work to create the first supranational institution in contemporary European history laid the foundations for a union of Europe's countries. Today they are viewed as the founding fathers of the European Union, and Europe Day is now celebrated every year on 9 May, the date in 1950 when Schuman delivered his landmark speech on the creation of the ECSC.

INITIAL FAILURES

This period was also marked by the Cold War, as tensions between the two blocs reached their peak and the Western bloc felt compelled to organise the rearmament of the Federal Republic of Germany, which found itself vulnerable to the threat posed by the Soviet Union. The French government believed that it was imperative for this rearmament to be managed by a European body with the power to control Germany's military production. Consequently, alongside the Schuman Plan, Monnet introduced a long-term plan to create a European army under the control of a supranational defence ministry.

With the support of René Pleven (1901-1993), the president of the Council of Ministers under whose name the plan would become known, this project led to the signature of the treaty creating the European Defence Community (EDC), which was placed under the control of NATO, in May 1952. However, the treaty was never ratified due to French opposition to any kind of German militarisation, which led the country's National Assembly to reject the plan following an intense period of debates and anti-EDC campaigns. At the same time, France also rejected a proposal to create a European Political Community (EPC), whose role would be to define a shared foreign policy for all the countries of Europe. This constituted a painful defeat for Monnet, who resigned as President of the High Authority of the ECSC.

However, other leading figures, including Schuman and Spaak, understood the importance of drawing lessons from this defeat to prevent the same problems from arising in the future. Specifically, they concluded that the European nations were not yet prepared to countenance political integration, so the European community should be built through economic cooperation.

THE CREATION OF THE EUROPEAN ECONOMIC COMMUNITY: A KEY TURNING POINT

Monnet and Spaak then worked on a project for economic cooperation which aimed to gradually establish a common market and envisaged the possibility of creating a joint organisation for research on nuclear power for civilian use. This was followed by discussions in all the countries involved, and the Messina Conference (1 to 3 June 1955) resulted in the creation of a committee comprising experts and ministerial delegates in order to consider the issue and produce a report on a customs union to be led by Spaak. In summer 1956, negotiations took place between the governments of Europe so that a treaty could be drafted.

The Treaty of Rome was signed on 25 March 1957 by the member states of the ECSC, namely the Federal Republic of Germany, Belgium, the Netherlands, Luxembourg, France and Italy, and led to the creation of the European Economic Community (EEC). It paved the way for the setting up of a customs union and the implementation of the rules needed for it to run smoothly, the creation of a joint nuclear research association (Euratom) and the introduction of institutions to promote social integration. The EEC comprised three bodies:

- The **Council of the European Communities**, whose presidency alternated between representatives of each of the member states. It produced directives (recommendations for the member states) and regulations (laws which the member states had to obey). Initially, decisions were taken by unanimity, but the plan was for them to be taken by majority vote after a transition period.

- The **Commission of the European Communities**, which proposed measures to the Council.
- The **Assembly**, which comprised 142 members and was intended to represent the interests of the European people.

The EEC also inherited the Court of Justice, which was created with the ECSC.

The Treaty of Rome was an important step in the history of the construction of the European Union. While the project of a political union was abandoned after the failure of the EDC and EPC, economic integration looked like a promising approach, and the EEC brought progress towards greater supranationalism. However, although this was a step forward in terms of closer European integration, progress towards greater cooperation in Europe was shaky in the years that followed.

THE FIRST SETBACKS IN THE CONSTRUCTION OF THE EUROPEAN UNION (1960-1969)

Failure to expand

The 1960s saw important shifts in the European political landscape. The OEEC, which had previously been deemed obsolete, was modernised and given greater powers, becoming the Organisation for Economic Cooperation and Development (OECD). In 1965, the EEC decided to merge the institutions of the ECSC, the EEC and the Council of Europe to create a single Council of Ministers and Commission (both based in Brussels) and a single assembly, the European Parliament (located in Strasbourg). Luxembourg was now home to the administrative services and the European Court of Justice.

At the same time, Charles de Gaulle, whom Jean Monnet viewed as an opponent of a united Europe, became President of France. Indeed, although de Gaulle was not wholly against the idea of European cooperation, he firmly rejected supranationalism. Instead, he wanted Europe to be comprised of a group of independent nations and for France to retain absolute national sovereignty and even a certain degree of precedence. That said, he advocated greater cooperation through the Fouchet Plan in June 1961. However, although the plan was redrafted repeatedly, France and its neighbours could not reach an agreement, as de Gaulle viewed the other European nations' plans as too federalist.

A key topic of discussion during the negotiations was the membership of the economically powerful United Kingdom. Indeed, the successes of the common market proved a tempting prospect for the UK government, which did not want to be left isolated and shut out of the decision-making centre which was taking shape in mainland Europe. Consequently, in February 1962, the UK applied to join the organisation and expressed its desire to open discussions on its membership. However, the talks soon ran into obstacles, particularly the UK's request to be exempt from the regulations fixing customs duties so as not to compromise its favourable trading relationship with the rest of the Commonwealth countries, and its opposition to the EEC's

Common Agricultural Policy (CAP). The CAP was the Community's main centre of investment and intervened to maintain fixed prices for agricultural products in all member countries. However, these fixed prices were higher than prices in the UK at that time, which was a major problem.

Given these serious stumbling blocks, Charles de Gaulle immediately rejected the UK's candidacy on the grounds that all member states must respect the organisation's rules in their entirety. However, his real fear was the entry into the EEC of a country that was strong enough to compete with France. In January 1963, the UK's candidacy was rejected, due in large part to vehement opposition from France.

Nonetheless, the UK was undeterred by this rejection and applied again in April 1967. Although the members of the EEC were generally in favour of its accession, de Gaulle would not budge, justifying his stance with the same reasons as the first time round. The UK government then suggested a partnership with the EEC without full membership, but de Gaulle demanded complete adhesion or nothing.

The empty chair crisis

In 1966, a new mode of decision-making, in line with the provisions of the Treaty of Rome (1957), was introduced in the Council of the EEC: from now on, decisions would be based on a majority vote rather than on unanimity. De Gaulle viewed this change as unacceptable because it would strengthen the supranational character of the EEC institutions, thus jeopardising France's hopes of greater political influence and sparking fears that measures threatening its national sovereignty would be imposed. One year earlier, a bill to revise the CAP funding procedures and to grant greater powers to the Commission had been passed in the Parliament. Although France was committed to the CAP, de Gaulle was not prepared to accept the institutional reforms that the other member states wanted to accompany it. This engendered divisions to which no real solution was found.

On 1 July 1965, the French representatives to the European institutions were recalled, meaning that they no longer took part in Council meetings. This led to what became known as the "empty chair crisis". Although the text concerning the

CAP was modified, France stuck to its policy and the crisis lasted for six months. There were two main reasons for the stalemate: firstly, France was opposed to the Commission being granted increased powers, and secondly, de Gaulle was trying to prevent the introduction of majority decision-making.

The conflict was resolved in January 1966 thanks to the Luxembourg Compromise. As its name suggests, this was not an official treaty, but rather a consensus according to which the members of the EEC had an informal right to veto on certain matters of national interest (although what exactly constituted a matter of national interest was not clearly defined), allowing France to continue opposing legislation or decisions that it did not agree with.

FURTHER EXPANSION (1969-1989)

An encouraging revival

Charles de Gaulle stepped down as President of France on 27 April 1969 and was replaced by Georges Pompidou (1911-1974) on 15 June of the same year, raising hopes of a way out of the impasse the EEC found itself in. On 21 October 1969, Willy Brandt (1913-1992) became Chancellor of the Federal Republic of Germany, which also boded well for the revival of the construction of a united Europe, as, like Pompidou, Brandt was a firm believer in the importance of this project. Indeed, although Pompidou shared de Gaulle's opinions on many matters, he was not opposed to the UK's accession to the EEC.

The situation was resolved at The Hague Summit on 1 and 2 December 1969 when, on Brandt's initiative, 1 July 1970 was set as the deadline for negotiations for the four candidate countries to the EEC (the UK, Ireland, Denmark and Norway). Furthermore, from 1970 onwards the six existing member countries began to cooperate more closely and sometimes consulted each other on matters of foreign policy.

Following extensive negotiations, the new candidacies were accepted by the EEC's members. In 1972, the House of Commons in the UK ratified the accession treaty, while referendums in Ireland and Denmark favoured accession. However, in Norway 54% of voters opposed membership of the EEC. Consequently, from 19 to 21 October the nine member states of the EEC met at the Paris Summit to discuss the future of budgetary cooperation.

The official accession of the three new member states in May 1973 resulted in major changes in the EEC. The election of Valéry Giscard d'Estaing, a firm supporter of the European project, as President of France in May 1974 allowed a number of long-standing problems to be resolved. As such, the summit held in Paris on 9 and 10 December 1974 was an important step forward. The attendees decided to establish the European Council, which would bring together the leaders of member states once or twice per year. Working groups were also created to reflect on sub-national rights for citizens of EEC countries. Finally, in 1979 direct universal suffrage for the election of Members of the European Parliament was introduced.

The strength of the Franco-German partnership and progress in the 1980s

The political outlook in the early 1980s was bleak: on the global stage, tensions between West and East were constantly rising, particularly following the Soviet invasion of Afghanistan in 1979. Within Europe, the situation was not much better, and the UK was proving reluctant to contribute its share to the joint budget, which resulted in discord within the EEC.

However, things began to look up in 1985, when Portugal and Spain joined the EEC. They had both been candidates since 1977 and had recently emerged from the shadows of dictatorship, which smoothed the way to their accession. Accession treaties were signed in Madrid and Lisbon on 12 June 1985 and quickly ratified. On 1 January 1986, the two countries officially became EEC member states and gained access to the European economic system.

The elections of Helmut Kohl as Chancellor of the Federal Republic of Germany and François Mitterrand as President of France in October 1982 gave the European project new momentum. In 1984, Mitterrand expressed his support for the European Parliament's proposal of the more extensive use of the majority vote system, thus putting an end to the French stonewalling that had begun with Charles de Gaulle. Furthermore, when the European Council met on 25 and

26 June 1984, most European leaders expressed their support for the drafting of a foundational document of a major political entity, the European Union, by a committee of experts. Only the UK, Denmark and Greece were reticent, as they saw this as a worrying step towards supranationalism. In spite of their opposition, the European Parliament took steps to develop this proposal and put it into practice. Mitterrand and Kohl threw their weight behind the initiative and influenced the European Council in Luxembourg in its decision to draft a text making provisions for the revision of the Treaty of Rome in order to expand political and economic cooperation. The Single European Act (SEA), which was signed in Luxembourg and The Hague on 17 and 28 February 1986 by the foreign ministers of each member state, relaxed international borders and made plans for a monetary union, although it did not set out a precise timeline for the latter. This Act was set to come into effect on 1 January 1993, in conjunction with the creation of the European Union.

A committee of experts led by the French Minister of Finance Jacques Delors (born in 1925) was tasked with exploring these issues in more detail. The committee's report was published on 17 April 1989 and set out three recommended phases, but there was no specific deadline for any of them. The first step was to strengthen the European Monetary System (EMS), which oversaw European currencies to prevent major fluctuations in their values. It would then be necessary to coordinate the values of the currencies of the various member states and create a European Central Bank. The final recommendation was the adoption of a single currency. While Belgium, France and Italy supported this plan, the Federal Republic of Germany was concerned that the single currency could prove less stable than the Deutsche Mark and the UK rejected the idea outright. In spite of these disagreements, a consensus was reached and the first phase was scheduled, although this did not imply a firm commitment to the other two steps of the project.

Over the course of the 1980s, the EEC's plans to form a monetary union and remove internal borders began to take shape. However, the fall of the Berlin Wall in 1989 led the Community to turn its attention in a new direction, as Eastern Europe now offered interesting prospects.

FROM THE EEC TO THE EU (1989-2004)

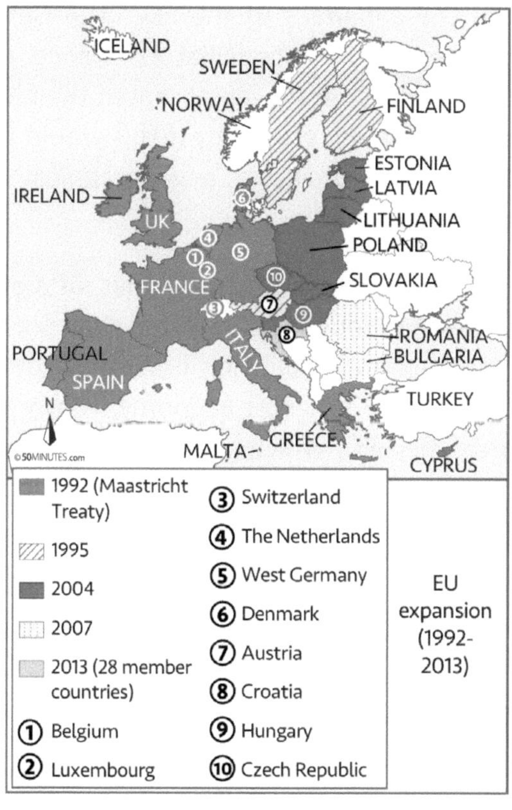

Eastern Europe: a new horizon

At the Strasbourg European Summit in 1989, the European Council affirmed its support for German reunification, which finally took place on 3 October 1990, resulting in an unprecedented shift in the dynamics of the EEC. The German government took a conciliatory stance on a number of issues and even accepted the idea of a monetary union, especially if this would bring about the first phase of a geographical shift towards the East.

From 1990 onwards, the countries of Central and Eastern Europe (CEE) rejected their socialist governments and took their first steps towards democracy and a market economy. They turned towards the EEC, which was expanding to the East and welcoming these nascent democracies into the fold. From 1989 onwards, the "Demosthenes" programme, which was set up to support the former Eastern bloc countries in their transition to democracy, encouraged the CEE countries to meet the necessary standards for EEC membership. At the same time, the European Council created the so-called special guest status, which allowed these countries (notably Hungary and Poland) to send delegates to the Council. These delegates could not vote, but they were allowed to take part in the Council's work.

The creation of the European Union

A series of intergovernmental conferences in 1990 led to the consensus that the biggest supporters of European cooperation had been hoping for since the earliest initiatives in the aftermath of the Second World War.

The Maastricht Treaty, which was signed on 7 February 1992, modified previous agreements and created a European Union. At this stage, the Union comprised 12 countries, had institutions with limited supranational powers and was in favour of both expansion and further development in existing sectors, as these two goals were seen as linked. The treaty's ambitious goals were based on three pillars: a European Community and its constituent sectors of activity, shared foreign policy, and cooperation in terms of legislation and law enforcement.

The treaty also extended the Community's areas

of activity to encompass research and industry, and tasked it with working on closer political coordination. From this point on, the European institutions could intervene in education, professional training, health, culture and consumer protection. Plans were also made for a Common Foreign and Security Identity (CFSI) linked to a union of the Western European countries, with the support of NATO, which would serve as the armed forces of the organisation. The treaty further recalled the key goals of the preservation of peace and protection of human rights. Moreover, it made provisions to establish European citizenship, which would give all European citizens the right to move freely across the continent, vote in European elections and live in any other member state. With regard to judicial cooperation, emphasis was placed on fighting crime at the EU's outer borders. Finally, the treaty confirmed the creation of a monetary union and made plans for the introduction of a single currency.

After some disagreements, the treaty was ratified by all member states on 2 August 1992 and entered into force on 1 January 1993. After challenging negotiations with the UK and

Denmark, it was agreed that they were not obligated to continue to the third phase of the EMU and adopt the single currency.

The EU-15 and the monetary union

By the time the Maastricht Treaty was signed, there were four new candidates for accession: Finland, Sweden, Norway and Austria. All these countries met the conditions for membership, as set out in the European Council meeting held in Lisbon in 1992, and the 12 members of the young European Union viewed their accession as a promising step forward. Indeed, these four countries were all developed, with relatively low populations and high GDPs, which would allow them to make a sizeable contribution to the Community budget. The candidate countries, for their part, were drawn to the prospect of a common market and their desire to be involved in decision-making at the European level.

The accession treaties were signed in Corfu on 24 June 1994, triggering the ratification phase, which necessitated a referendum. Austria was the first country to vote because its citizens were deemed most favourable to EU membership, which could encourage the inhabitants of the other three countries to vote the same way. In fact, ratification went without a hitch in Austria, Sweden and Finland, and preparations to join the monetary union got underway immediately. However, 52.2% of Norwegian citizens voted against the country's accession. On 1 January 1995, the other candidates officially acceded to the EU, which now counted 15 member states and 370 million inhabitants.

In subsequent years, the programme to strengthen relations between EU countries slowed somewhat. In 1995, France stated that it could no longer guarantee free movement in line with the 1985 Schengen Agreement because of the need to safeguard its domestic security and combat terrorism. The Schengen Area, which was originally conceived by the Federal Republic of Germany, France, Belgium, Luxembourg and the Netherlands, proved difficult to implement because of the distrust that some member states harboured towards their neighbours. However, in 1996 France ended up accepting the programme. At this time, the Schengen Area encompassed 13 EU member states (Germany,

France, Belgium, the Netherlands, Luxembourg, Austria, Denmark, Spain, Portugal, Sweden, Italy, Greece and Finland) and two non-EU countries (Iceland and Norway).

1999 was a pivotal year in the construction of the European Union, as it saw the first attempts to implement a Common Security and Defence Policy (CSDF), the successor to the CSDI, as well as the launch of the euro, the single European currency that marked the culmination of the monetary union project first proposed by Jacques Delors in 1989. The UK, Denmark and Sweden opted not to participate, while Greece was excluded because it did not meet the convergence criteria.

Europe's leaders viewed the launch of the single currency as a major step forward. It was adopted by Greece on 1 January 2001, and Sweden and Denmark held referendums on the subjects. However, in both cases their citizens rejected the euro. From 2002 onwards, the euro reached and then surpassed dollar parity. However, the international economic crisis meant that a number of EU member states, including France, Spain and Greece, could not maintain the balance imposed by the European Central Bank.

THE 2000S: A NEW ORDER

Towards a European Constitution

The European Council meeting held in Cologne in 1999 adopted Germany's idea of setting up a committee to draw up a Charter of Fundamental Rights of the European Union.

The Charter transmitted to the member states in December 2000 was ambitious in that it advocated close ties between all the EU countries and established a list of shared values, divided into six categories: human dignity, fundamental freedoms, equal rights, solidarity, European citizenship and equal, equitable justice. While the Council recognised the validity of these propositions, the Charter was not binding.

At the same time, plans were being made for an EU constitution. On 12 May 2000, the German foreign minister Joschka Fischer (born in 1948) expressed his support for the long-term development of a true European federation. The French president Jacques Chirac (born in 1932) responded by accepting a proposal to draw up a European constitution on 27 June 2000.

The European Council delegated this task to a committee headed by Valéry Giscard d'Estaing. Between February 2002 and June 2003, this committee worked on a constitutional text, which was subsequently presented to the Council. The text incorporated the Charter drawn up in 2000 and laid the foundations for a much broader programme. Although the European institutions approved the new constitution in 2004, it did not enter into force because it was not ratified by all member states; specifically, the citizens of France and the Netherlands rejected it in their respective referendums. This constituted a further failure in the ongoing attempts to strengthen the political union.

Towards the EU-28: new challenges (2004-2013)

The early years of the new millennium marked a further turning point for the European Union. 1 May 2004 saw the biggest enlargement in EU history, with the accession of ten new countries (Estonia, Hungary, Latvia, Lithuania, Malta,

Cyprus, Poland, the Czech Republic, Slovakia and Slovenia), taking the total number of member states from 15 to 25. Furthermore, the new countries were not Western European, meaning that this expansion surpassed the scope of the union as projected by the first pro-Europe leaders in the aftermath of the Second World War. This was soon followed by more accessions: Bulgaria and Romania joined the EU on 1 January 2007, and Croatia became a member on 1 July 2013.

In the wake of this expansion and strengthening of ties, anti-Europe movements proliferated and became increasingly prominent. This Euroscepticism took different forms and arose for different reasons depending on the country, but was generally linked to a feeling of subjugation. For example, France's Front National, led by Marine Le Pen (French politician, born in 1968), viewed the strengthening of the European Union as an unacceptable assault on the country's national sovereignty. This feeling was shared by the Belgian far-right party Vlaams Belang, whose criticism of the European project was tied to its nationalist and separatist sentiments. Some Eurosceptics, such as Geert Wilders (born in 1963), the founder of the Dutch Party for Freedom, who has demanded the abolition of the European Parliament, have been particularly virulent in their criticism of the EU and painted it as a virtual dictatorship.

The new EU member states, which had only recently obtained their independence from the USSR, seemed to prefer an intergovernmental union and appeared disinclined to accept greater supranationalism. Furthermore, it looked as though the EU would have to adapt its institutions and functioning, as they had been developed at a time when there were far fewer member states.

After the failure to ratify the EU constitution, the member states turned their attention to a new solution. On 13 December 2007, the 27 EU countries signed the Treaty of Lisbon, which came into force in 2009 and updated the workings of the European institutions. This treaty forms the basis of the functioning of the EU today.

THE EU TODAY

The EU currently comprises seven official institutions, which each have their own functions and responsibilities:

- The **European Council.** This is made up of the leaders of member states, who meet every six months in Brussels. They define the EU's political priorities and the general direction it should take. This is also where the most sensitive problems are dealt with, making the European Council the highest supranational level of the EU. It is led by a president, who is elected for a two-year term.
- The **European Parliament.** This comprises a maximum of 751 MEPs (including the president) who meet 12 times per year. MEPs are elected by direct universal suffrage every five years. The Parliament decides on the content of European legislation in agreement with the Council, oversees the entry of new member states and the work of the Commission, and is responsible for approving the Community budget. It also examines the agenda of European Council meetings and the reports

from the Commission in order to ensure the democratic functioning of these institutions.

- The **European Commission.** This is tasked with implementing the Community budget and granting European financing. It also presents legislative proposals to the European Parliament and the European Council. It comprises 28 Commissioners (one per member state) whose responsibilities are delegated by the president, who is selected by the European Council. This process is subject to oversight by the Parliament. Furthermore, the Commission represents the EU in international diplomacy. It meets at least once per week in Brussels or Luxembourg.

- The **Council of the European Union.** Not to be confused with the European Council or the Council of Europe, which is not an EU institution, the Council of the European Union is tasked with adopting Community legislation and approving the Community budget, in agreement with the European Parliament. It is also in charge of coordinating economic policy and the shared defence policy. Finally, the Council of the European Union must ensure that justice is uniformly and fairly applied in all member states and monitor politicians' behaviour in the fight against crime and terrorism. The members of this institution are not fixed; in each session, the member states are represented by the government minister whose responsibilities correspond to the subject at hand.

- The **Court of Justice.** This comprises 28 judges (one per member state) and nine Advocate Generals, each of whom are appointed for six-year terms. The Court delivers rulings on matters concerning member states and their obligations and rules on complaints lodged against the EU by countries, private organisations or individuals.
- The **Court of Auditors.** This monitors the use of EU funds and provides the Parliament with reports on Community finances, which the Parliament takes into account before it approves any budgets. The Court of Auditors can detect fraud but cannot punish it, so it must pass any suspected fraud cases on to the European Anti-Fraud Office.
- The **European Central Bank.** This monitors the stability of prices and the financial system as a whole within the EU. The president of the

ECB is selected by the leaders of the member states and coordinates the central banks of these countries.

In addition, the EU has its own administrative services, which consume around 6% of its annual budget. As of early 2018, there were around 33 000 people working in the European Commission, around 7500 in the European Parliament and 3500 in the Council of the European Union.

The future of the EU is currently looking less certain that it once did, following the UK's unprecedented decision to withdraw from the organisation. This sparked fears that other countries could follow suit, particularly with the rise of increasingly vocal and influential Eurosceptic parties such as Marine Le Pen's National Front in France and Geert Wilders' Party for Freedom in the Netherlands. However, both these parties failed to gain power in their respective elections in 2017. At present, the increasingly illiberal and repressive regimes in Poland and Hungary are causing concern, and it remains to be seen how the EU will surmount this challenge.

SUMMARY

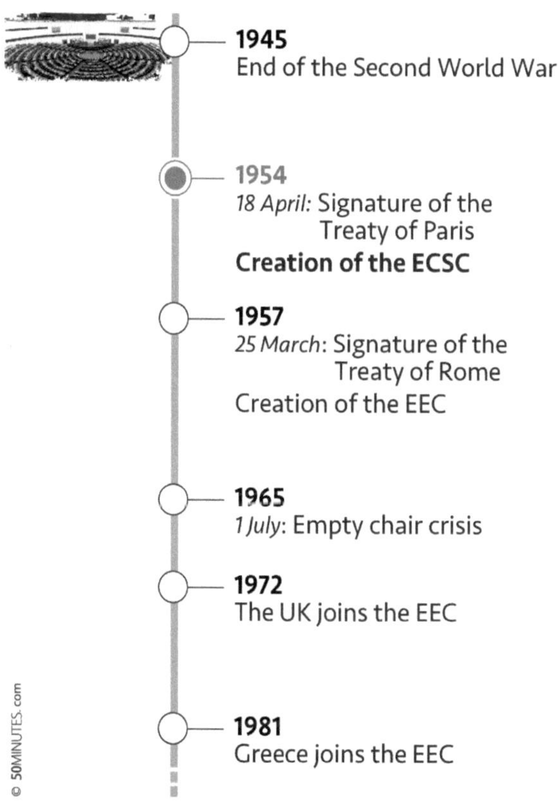

1945
End of the Second World War

1954
18 April: Signature of the
Treaty of Paris
Creation of the ECSC

1957
25 March: Signature of the
Treaty of Rome
Creation of the EEC

1965
1 July: Empty chair crisis

1972
The UK joins the EEC

1981
Greece joins the EEC

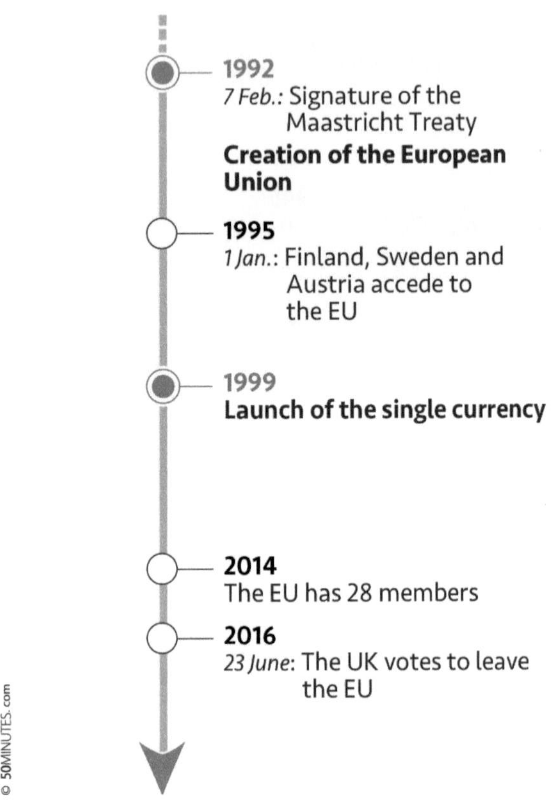

- After the Second World War, the first steps towards greater European unity were taken with the aim of stimulating recovery and guaranteeing lasting peace in the war-torn continent. The USA, which was eager to secure allies against the increasingly powerful USSR, provided economic support for these projects.

- On 18 April 1954, the signature of the Treaty of Paris created the European Coal and Steel Community (ECSC), the first supranational organisation in modern Europe.

- On 25 March 1957, the Treaty of Rome was signed by the members of the ECSC (the Federal Republic of Germany, Belgium, Luxembourg, the Netherlands, France and Italy), creating the European Economic Community (EEC).

- The 1960s were marked by reluctance on the part of the countries of Europe to accept increased supranationalism. Further stumbling blocks were the rejection of the UK's two attempts to join the EEC and the empty chair crisis caused by the French president Charles de Gaulle.

- The 1970s saw renewed progress towards closer cooperation. The French president Georges Pompidou and the German Chancellor Willy Brandt put aside their countries' past differences to work together, and in 1972 the UK joined the EEC, followed by Ireland and Denmark.

- The 1980s, which were marked by heightened

Cold War tensions, saw increased European cooperation, driven largely by the French president François Mitterrand and Germany's Helmut Kohl. Greece joined the EEC in 1981, followed by Portugal and Spain four years later.

- The late 1980s were a key turning point: as Communist regimes collapsed in Eastern Europe and Germany was reunified, European integration was focused on the East for the first time.
- The Maastricht Treaty, signed on 7 February 1992, created the European Union. This strengthened cooperation between the body's member states and paved the way for further enlargement. On 1 January 1995, Finland, Sweden and Austria acceded to the EU.
- In 1999, the introduction of a single currency, namely the euro, heralded the start of a new era in the European project.
- The countries of Eastern Europe began to join the EU: Estonia, Latvia, Lithuania, Hungary, Poland, the Czech Republic, Malta, Slovakia, Slovenia and Cyprus acceded in 2004, followed by Bulgaria and Romania in 2007 and Croatia in 2013, taking the total number of member

states to 28.

- On 23 June 2016, the citizens of the United Kingdom voted to leave the EU, the first time a nation has made this decision since its inception. Article 50 of the Treaty on the European Union was invoked the following year, and the UK is due to leave the EU in March 2019.

We want to hear from you!
Leave a comment on your online library
and share your favourite books on social media!

FIND OUT MORE

BIBLIOGRAPHY

- Abélès, M. (1992) *La vie quotidienne au Parlement européen*. Paris: Hachette.

- Bitsch, M-T. (2004) *Histoire de la construction européenne de 1945 à nos jours*. Paris: Éditions Complexe.

- Bossuat, G. (1994) *Les fondateurs de l'Europe*. Paris: Belin.

- Coutron, L., Gaillard, M. and Tronquoy, P. (2004) *L'Union européenne et le projet de Constitution*. Paris: La Documentation française.

- Dumoulin, M., Duchenne, G. and Van Laer, A. (2003) *La Belgique, les petits États et la construction européenne*. Brussels: Peter Lang.

- Official website of the European Union: <https://europa.eu/european-union/index_en>

KEY BUILDINGS

The buildings listed below are all open to visitors.

- The Court of Justice of the European Union in

Luxembourg.

- The European Central Bank in Frankfurt.

- The European Commission in Brussels.

- The European Council in Brussels.

- The European Court of Auditors in Luxembourg.

- The European Parliament in Brussels, Luxembourg and Strasbourg.

www.50minutes.com

Ebook EAN: 9782806289759

Paperback EAN: 9782806289766

Legal Deposit: D/2016/12603/772

Cover: © Primento

Digital conception by Primento, the digital partner of publishers.